Science
and
Sustainable Water

Stuart A. Kallen

ReferencePoint
Press®

San Diego, CA

© 2018 ReferencePoint Press, Inc.
Printed in the United States

For more information, contact:
ReferencePoint Press, Inc.
PO Box 27779
San Diego, CA 92198
www.ReferencePointPress.com

LIBRARY OF CONGRESS CATALOGING-IN-PUBLICATION DATA

Names: Kallen, Stuart A., 1955– author.
Title: Science and Sustainable Water/by Stuart A. Kallen.
Description: San Diego, CA: ReferencePoint Press, Inc., [2018] | Series:
    Science and Sustainability series | Audience: Grades 9-12. | Includes
    bibliographical references and index.
Identifiers: LCCN 2017014676 (print) | LCCN 2017018800 (ebook) | ISBN
    9781682822586 (eBook) | ISBN 9781682822579 (hardback)
Subjects: LCSH: Water-supply—Juvenile literature. |
    Water—Purification—Juvenile literature.
Classification: LCC TD348 (ebook) | LCC TD348 .K363 2018 (print) | DDC
    628.1--dc23
LC record available at https://lccn.loc.gov/2017014676

CONTENTS

INTRODUCTION

Sustainable Water

> **"Go to a faucet. Turn it on. This—water flowing out, clean, drinkable, always-on—this is the lifeblood of society."**
>
> —Alexis C. Madrigal, journalist at the *Atlantic*
>
> Alexis C. Madrigal, "American Aqueduct: The Great California Water Saga," *Atlantic*, February 24, 2014. www.theatlantic.com.

A human being cannot live more than three days without water. Without a constant supply of fresh, clean water, civilization would collapse. But most people do not give this life-sustaining resource a second thought. According to a 2016 HuffPost/YouGov poll, 45 percent of Americans said they did not understand where the water in their homes came from or how it was treated. Only 21 percent said they understood the workings of their water supply "very well." Despite this lack of knowledge, 71 percent said they were confident that their community water supply was safe.

The high level of confidence in America's water supply is not misplaced. There are approximately 155,000 public water systems in the United States, and they supply over 260 million Americans with quality water 24 hours a day, 365 days a year. According to water safety expert Hubert Colas, "That's quite a feat and we take that for granted."[1] This feat is made possible by a multitude of biologists, chemists, and other scientists who produce water that is palatable (pleasant tasting) and potable (safe to drink).

One of the most important jobs of a water treatment scientist is to ensure tap water is free of contamination that can affect public health. Scientists use various processes to remove heavy metals, industrial solvents, fecal coliform bacteria, and viruses and other pathogens from a water system. Failure to remove these substances from the water supply can have both short- and long-term consequences. The presence of bacteria like E. coli can cause immediate public health problems such as widespread outbreak of cramps, nausea, diarrhea, headaches, and more. Heavy metals such as lead and arsenic and industrial chemicals like benzene can lead to an increased risk of cancer, reproductive problems, and learning disorders.

A Drop in the Bucket

Water covers 70 percent of the earth, which leads many people to think water is plentiful. But 98 percent of the water on earth is seawater, which is 3.5 percent salt. Seawater is undrinkable, and when consumed, the high salt content creates a chemical imbalance in the body that can lead to massive dehydration and death. Additionally, salt water cannot be consumed by most land plants and animals, making it useless for agriculture.

Only about 2 percent of water on earth is freshwater, but most of that is frozen, locked up in ice caps and glaciers. Freshwater available for human use—water found in lakes, rivers, streams, and underground deposits called aquifers—makes up less than 0.5 percent of all the water on the planet. Looking at the numbers another way, if all the water on earth could fit in a 1-gallon (3.8-L) bucket, only about 1 tablespoon (15 ml) would be liquid freshwater.

This relatively small amount of earth's water has been used and reused by plants and animals for millions of years. It flows into rivers, lakes, and oceans as snow and rain and evaporates back into the atmosphere to become precipitation that falls again in a never-ending cycle.

> **WORDS IN CONTEXT**
>
> **aquifer**
> Sponge-like gravel- and sand-filled underground reservoirs that contain naturally occurring freshwater.

Along the way the water flows through the bodies of billions of people, animals, and plants. But earth's freshwater supply is endangered. It is increasingly contaminated by salts, metals, chemicals, and other matter. This decline leads scientists to formulate

new solutions to deal with worldwide water shortages. They are inventing new water conservation technologies, such as recycling wastewater, and developing energy-efficient facilities to desalinate, or remove salt from, seawater. Researchers are using nanotechnology and other cutting-edge sciences to clean up water pollution.

The Most Important Endeavor

According to the United Nations, each person needs at least 13 gallons (50 L) of water a day to drink, wash, prepare meals, and maintain personal hygiene. However, a 2015 World Wildlife Fund study showed that about 1.1 billion people, about 15 percent of the world's population, lack access to this basic amount of fresh-water. Another 2.7 billion, more than one-third of all people on earth, live in places where water is scarce at least one month a year.

Beyond personal needs, freshwater is critical to agriculture and industry. It takes more than 2,400 gallons (9,085 L) of water to produce 1 pound (454 g) of meat. The production of a typical smartphone requires 240 gallons (908 L) of water.

Stanley Weiner, chief executive officer of the desalination company STW Resources, emphasizes the importance of making water sustainable: "Water is behind every single sector of our economy and our way of life. . . . It's important that everyone understands that finding a solution for our growing water crisis is hands-down the most important endeavor of our time—from both a human and an industrial standpoint."[2]

CHAPTER ONE

The Science of Freshwater

> "Safe, healthy drinking water is one of those things [people] take for granted. It's always there when you need it, yet you rarely think about how incredible that is."

—Mariia Lvovych, water consultant

Mariia Lvovych, "Is It Actually Safe to Drink? Understanding Which Factors Impact Water Quality and the Perception of Healthy Drinking Water," Frontiers, August 26, 2015. www.frontiersin.org.

Scientists rarely make headlines—especially scientists who specialize in studying the aging waterworks in crumbling American cities. But in 2015 environmental engineer Marc Edwards participated in several televised news conferences. His words were featured in dozens of news articles throughout the world. Edwards was the principal investigator of a major water crisis unfolding in Flint, Michigan.

In early 2015 Edwards discovered unsafe levels of lead in the tap water flowing into thousands of homes in Flint. Lead is a heavy metal that in high levels can be toxic to the human body. Edwards found that in many cases the amount of lead in the water was over 130 times higher than levels considered safe by the US Environmental Protection Agency (EPA). The water was also contaminated with bacteria that turned it brownish yellow, gave it a foul taste, and made it smell like rotten eggs.

The contaminants in the water quickly started afflicting nearly every Flint resident who drank or washed with city water. Symptoms of lead poisoning were particularly noticeable in hundreds of children. They developed rashes, their eyelashes fell out, they had severe cramps, and their growth was stunted. Flint resident Melissa Mays describes how the tainted water harmed her and her three young sons:

> The biggest thing was rashes, bumpy and lumpy. . . . You couldn't put makeup or lotion or anything over it—it burned when you touched it. It feels like a chemical burn on our faces, backs, and arms. There was nothing I could do to soothe it. . . . My kids were complaining of muscle and bone pain. I was feeling it, too. Our arms hurt, our bones hurt. . . . It turns out lead makes your bones weak.[3]

Lead also causes harm to the developing brains of children, lowering the IQ and causing attention disorders and behavioral problems.

The CSI of Plumbing

Edwards is an environmental engineer; he uses chemistry, biology, and other scientific principles to study how human activities impact the environment. He has also been called a science detective because he works with water utilities across the country to solve problems with corroding pipes and contamination in water supplies. Edwards sometimes describes his job in TV terms— a crime scene investigator, or CSI, of plumbing. It did not take Edwards long to solve the mystery of Flint's contaminated water. The problem was the result of chemistry.

Flint's water pipes, which were laid in the early 1900s, were made from lead and cast iron. For decades the city bought its drinking water from Detroit. Flint had a local water treatment plant, but it sat idle. The Detroit water contained a chemical called orthophosphate. This substance maintained a protective mineral crust that prevented corrosion in Flint's lead pipes. In early 2014 the Detroit water utility that was supplying Flint raised its water prices around $5 million a year. To save money, Flint began using its local water treatment plant in April 2014. The local facility drew

Workers dig up old lead water pipes in Flint, Michigan, so that they can be replaced. In 2015, the water in the city was found to be dangerously contaminated due to inadequate treatment, which allowed it to absorb lead from the pipes.

water from the Flint River. When the city switched water supplies, it did not add orthophosphate. Edwards concluded that without the orthophosphate, the protective crust in the pipes dissolved, allowing lead and rust to leach into the water. As investigative journalist Alison Young explains, the Flint water "basically stripped the insides of pipes and sent torrents of particles and lead into people's homes."[4] Additionally, as the pipes corroded, the surfaces became a breeding ground for bacteria, which gave the water its putrid color, taste, and smell.

Flint residents had been complaining to government officials for months before Edwards arrived to test their water and discovered the source of the problem. City water managers then took steps to add orthophosphate to Flint's water supply, but it took about a year for the protective layer to build up in the pipes again. In January 2017 Michigan environmental officials announced that Flint water no longer had unsafe levels of lead and was safe to drink. However, many residents remained suspicious of the water coming from their taps and continued to drink bottled water. Ultimately, Flint's entire network of municipal lead and iron water pipes will need to be replaced, but the price tag is $50 billion. The city, and even the state of Michigan, does not have the money to pay for the job. And the problem goes beyond Flint; a 2015 investigation by USA Today showed that as many as two thousand water systems in the United States are contaminated with lead. As many as 7 million households in all fifty states are at risk for lead poisoning and other health issues.

Rainwater Chemistry

Most scientists who work with municipal water supplies do not receive much public attention. But as the crisis in Flint demonstrates, the central mission of water scientists is to protect public health. Chemists, biologists, and environmental engineers must provide an endless flow of high-quality drinking water to the public every day. The job of the water engineer is made more difficult by the fact that water is a universal solvent; it dissolves and mingles with more natural and synthetic chemicals and substances than any other liquid on earth.

Wherever water travels—through the ground, through plants, or through human bodies—it carries valuable minerals and nutrients. But water can also transmit harmful compounds, pollution, and bacteria. Water treatment plants are designed to work with the unique chemistry of water to maximize the good substances and eliminate the bad. Treatment facilities use filters, chemicals, and scientific procedures to remove large and small contaminants.

The water that flows from household taps begins in nature. Water evaporates and rises into the air when the sun heats the surface of rivers, lakes, reservoirs, and oceans. When the water vapor rises, it separates from salt, dirt, minerals, and other matter. In a self-renewing process, the water molecules cool, re-form, and return to liquid in the form of rain and snow. This natural process is why rainwater is safe to drink almost everywhere in the world (before it hits the ground). When water falls as precipitation, it flows across the land and returns to rivers, lakes, and oceans, or it seeps into aquifers.

When rainwater flows into waterways, it naturally picks up minerals found in rocks and soil. These minerals change the pH value of the water. The term *pH* stands for "potential of hydrogen" and represents a numeric scale of 1 to 14 that specifies whether a water-based solution is acidic, neutral, or alkaline. Solutions with low pH values, around 1 or 2, are highly acidic; lemon juice has a pH of 2.2. Acids have a relatively large number of hydrogen ions. A high pH value of 12 or 13 indicates a solution is alkaline, such as household ammonia or lye. Alkalis have fewer hydrogen ions.

Clean rainwater is slightly acidic, as it has a pH of 6.5. The limestone rock that is common throughout the United States changes the pH of precipitation. As rainwater and melted snow soak into limestone layers, the water absorbs substances such as gypsum, calcium, and magnesium. Water that is high in mineral content is alkaline and referred to as "hard." Alkaline water above pH 7.6 can cause numerous problems. It tastes bad, does not create soapsuds, and leaves damaging mineral deposits in equipment like cooling towers and water heaters.

Acidic water also causes problems. Rainwater becomes more acidic when exposed to air pollution. In areas where coal is burned to produce electricity, sulfur dioxide and nitrogen oxide are pumped into the atmosphere. These chemical compounds create what is called acid rain, which has a pH of 4.3. Acid rain kills trees, bushes, and other plants. Acidic water is also highly corrosive. It is unhealthy to drink and destroys the metal pipes that are part of the water distribution system.

What Is in the Water?

Freshwater is also affected by what is called nonpoint-source pollution. This type of pollution consists of contamination that

WATER: THE UNIVERSAL SOLVENT

Most people think of water as something to drink, bathe in, or clean with. A chemist, however, sees water as the chemical formula H_2O. H_2 represents two hydrogen atoms, while the O stands for one oxygen atom. Together, these three atoms create a water molecule. And this formula is also what gives water a unique property—it is a universal solvent.

A solvent is a substance that dissolves another substance. As a universal solvent, water can dissolve more substances than any other solvent on earth. When a substance dissolves in water, its molecules break down. For example, salt is known by the chemical name sodium chloride, or $NaCl$. When salt is added to water, the oxygen molecules attract sodium molecules, while water's hydrogen molecules attract chloride. Because these substances are broken down on a molecular level, an observer cannot see salt in salt water.

The idea of water as a universal solvent is connected to issues of water quality and the production of freshwater at water treatment plants. When it rains and snows, water flows into rivers, lakes, and aquifers. Along the way, water attracts and dissolves many substances in its path. These substances include natural minerals and synthetic elements, such as industrial and agricultural chemicals, personal care products, and pharmaceutical drugs. Scientists at water treatment plants must remove or neutralize all of the substances naturally absorbed by the universal solvent, water.

is widely dispersed from numerous sources in the environment. Nonpoint-source pollution includes bacteria, viruses, and other organisms. The bacteria known as E. coli is one of the most widely known biological toxins. E. coli is found in human and animal excrement. When it rains, E. coli enters waterways from agricultural feedlots and as runoff from lawns, streets, and storm drains.

Nonpoint-source pollutions also include motor oil, gasoline, antifreeze, and other toxic chemicals that leak onto roadways from cars and trucks. Industrial toxins enter the environment from mining operations, abandoned factories, and gas stations. All these pollutants wash into rivers, lakes, and aquifers when it rains or snows.

Agriculture is one of the largest contributors to nonpoint-source pollution. The United States has 330 million acres (133.5 million ha) of agricultural land that is treated with chemical fertilizers containing phosphorus, nitrogen, potassium, and other substances. When these fertilizers wash into waterways, they cause harmful algae blooms. Algae, sometimes referred to as pond scum, consists of microscopic organisms that float on the surface of the water. Just as fertilizer provides nutrients to corn and soybeans, it also makes algae grow but with negative results. Excessive amounts of algae consume oxygen in water and prevent sunlight from penetrating the surface. The lack of oxygen and light suffocates fish and kills other water creatures.

When fertilizers wash into waterways, they can cause algae to flourish in what is known as an algae bloom (pictured). Algae blooms choke off light and oxygen, killing fish and other living things that dwell in the water.

Agricultural land is also treated with massive amounts of chemical pesticides, including insecticides, herbicides, and fungicides. Pesticides, also used on golf courses, lawns and gardens, and forested areas, contaminate water and poison fish and wildlife. The United States produces over 1 billion pounds (454 million kg) of pesticides every year, and these poisons affect public health. Exposure to pesticides increases the risk of cancer, birth defects, and numerous other health problems.

Pollution and minerals make up what are called dissolved substances; their molecules are small enough that they can survive filtration in a water treatment plant. Other particles, known as suspensions, are larger than dissolved substances; suspensions are dispersed through water but are not dissolved. Suspensions are very tiny but can usually be seen with the naked eye or a microscope. Suspensions include tiny organisms such as algae, bacteria, and viruses. Suspensions, along with larger substances like silt and sand, impact the turbidity, or cloudiness of water.

> **WORDS IN CONTEXT**
>
> **suspensions**
> Particles that disperse through a solvent but do not dissolve.

Testing for Water Quality

Water quality varies with the seasons, depending on weather conditions and water levels. Large natural variations in water quality may be observed even in a single water source. Before water can be made potable, it must be investigated and evaluated to determine its quality. Scientists need to understand the composition of biological life in the water, the nature of particles (dissolved or suspended), and other physical characteristics. This evaluation is done through chemical analyses of water samples in a laboratory. Scientists take exact measurements of water temperature, pH, conductivity, light penetration, particle size of particulate material, and pollution levels.

Temperature testing determines the amount of dissolved oxygen in the water. Oxygen gas accumulates in water from the actions of the wind and waves and the movement of water over rocks, sand, and other obstacles in rivers and lakes. Cold water has more dissolved oxygen, making it a healthy environment for fish and other organisms. As water temperature increases, oxygen levels fall. If water is in the 70°F to 80°F range (21°C to 27°C), scientists would be on the lookout for algae, bacteria, and viruses, which thrive in oxygen-depleted water.

To test pH, scientists use a pH indicator, a chemical compound that is added to water and causes the liquid to change color depending on the amount of acid or alkali. Conductivity is a measure of water's ability to pass electrical current. Distilled water, which has zero dissolved minerals, does not conduct electricity. Water conductivity increases with the addition of minerals or

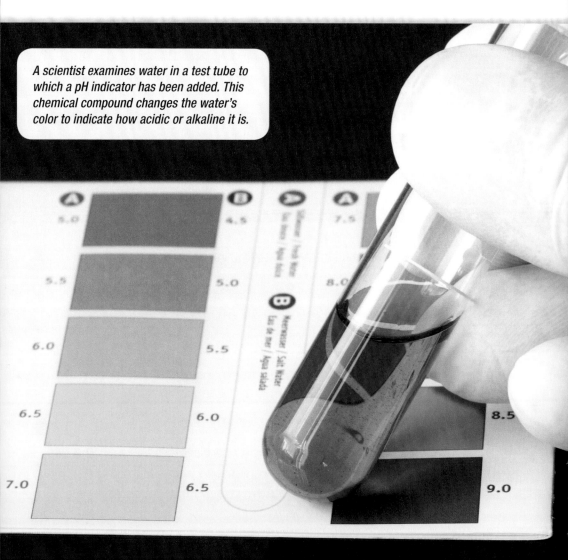

A scientist examines water in a test tube to which a pH indicator has been added. This chemical compound changes the water's color to indicate how acidic or alkaline it is.

chemicals. Salt water is a good conductor of electricity, as is hard water, which has many dissolved minerals. Scientists test conductivity with a simple tool called a multimeter, which checks for voltage and current. This test provides scientists a general sense of the total dissolved solid, indicating the chemical concentration in water without revealing the specific chemicals.

Nutrient testing establishes the amount of nitrogen present in the water. More nitrogen indicates more suspended algae and other aquatic plants. Heavy-metal testing helps scientists ascertain the amount of mercury, zinc, lead, and copper pollution that enters the water from industrial processes and mining.

Creating Purified Water

Engineers who operate treatment plants use the data taken from water samples as a basis for filtering and treating the drinking water that flows into homes and businesses. At the beginning of the process, water is pumped from rivers, lakes, and aquifers into water treatment facilities. During the primary treatment process, the water passes through screens made of thick steel bars about 2 inches (5 cm) apart that prevent brush, fish, branches, and other large objects from entering the facility's intake pipes. Smaller screens remove twigs and leaves. Once it is filtered, water may be diverted into a reservoir for a period lasting a few days to a few months. During this phase, a natural biological purification takes place. Living organisms such as aquatic plants, algae, snails, and helpful bacteria work together to consume sediment and some pollutants in the water.

> **WORDS IN CONTEXT**
>
> **turbidity**
>
> The clearness or cloudiness of a water sample.

Water managers test the turbidity and pH of the water before conducting the next steps in water purification, called the secondary treatment process. This procedure involves removing suspended and settled solids. The water is transferred to a large pool called a presedimentation basin. As the water sits in the basin, the force of gravity settles suspended solids like grit and sand to the bottom. The more turbid the water, the longer it sits in the basin. If water is too acidic, soda ash (sodium carbonate) or sodium hydroxide is added to raise the pH. If water is too alkaline, white vinegar or citric acid is added to balance the pH. In cities with lead and cast iron pipes, water managers add orthophosphate to prevent corrosion.

Fine particles such as dirt and algae, known as colloids, are not removed in the presedimentation basin. Gravity will not settle out these suspensions naturally because they are lighter than water. Colloids must be removed in a process known as coagulation and flocculation. A chemical called aluminum sulfate, or alum, is added to increase the weight of colloids. Mechanical mixers stir the alum into the water quickly in a process called rapid mix. The alum causes the particles to coagulate, or clump together into a semisolid substance. The water is then transferred to a basin, where it is gently stirred by slow-moving paddles. This stirring causes the coagulated particles to flocculate, or form into a large jellylike mass called floc.

Sometimes another chemical called powdered activated carbon is added during the coagulation-flocculation process. Powdered activated carbon is made from organic material such as charcoal. It is a highly porous material that absorbs bacteria and other compounds that can cause foul odors and unpleasant flavors in the water.

After flocculation the water and floc move to a sedimentation, or settling, basin. The water moves through the basin very slowly as gravity works to settle the floc to the bottom. Large rotating scrapers at the bottom of the basin push the floc into a large container called a hopper. The floc, now referred to as treatment residuals, must be emptied from the hopper several times a day.

After flowing out of the sedimentation basin, water is filtered through a bed of sand and gravel that is about 2 feet (61 cm) thick. As water passes through this natural filter, the remaining suspended particles are trapped in the sand. The filtered water is collected in pools called underdrains.

MEASURING TURBIDITY

One way environmental engineers assess drinking water quality is by measuring its turbidity, an optical determination of water clarity. The measurement of turbidity is provided by exposing a water sample to light rays to reveal the amount of clay, silt, microscopic organisms called plankton, and other fine particles. Light is absorbed by cloudy water; if the water is clear, light is transmitted through the sample in a straight line. A turbidity-testing device called a turbidimeter or nephelometer uses an incandescent light or a specialized light-emitting diode to illuminate a water sample from various angles. Light scatters, or is redirected, from its initial path as it bounces off small, suspended particles. A digital detector measures the percentage of light that is redirected. The more the light scatters, the more suspended particles are present in the water. Water scientists use the measurements provided by the turbidimeter to determine exactly how the water should be processed in a treatment plant.

In the final stage of the process, water is disinfected with chlorine—a chemical that kills microorganisms such as bacteria and viruses that can be found in reservoirs, water storage tanks, and water mains. These microorganisms can transmit diseases such as cholera, typhoid fever, dysentery, hepatitis, meningitis, and numerous other maladies that cause fever, vomiting, muscle aches, severe stomach and intestinal problems, and death. In about 75 percent of community water systems in the United States, the chemical fluoride—which protects against dental cavities—is also added in the final stage of water processing. The final product is pumped into pipes and transported to homes and businesses.

Millions of Gallons a Day

Water treatment plants operate around the clock every day of the year. The three treatment plants in Baltimore, Maryland, produce 405 million gallons (1.6 billion L) of clean drinking water every day for more than 2.7 million residents. The New York City water supply system provides 9.4 million residents with 1.3 billion gallons

(4.9 billion L) of clean, fresh drinking water daily. And the water is a great bargain. In 2015 the average American paid $2.50 for 600 gallons (2,271 L) of municipal water. This fee was about equal to the cost of 1 gallon (3.8 L) of bottled water purchased at the grocery store. And most tap water is as clean or cleaner than bottled water.

Unless there is a problem, few people ever consider the science behind their tap water. But as residents of Flint came to understand, when this vital resource is compromised, a public health crisis rapidly unfolds. Compromise is not an option when it comes to the chemistry and biology of freshwater. There are many contaminants lurking in the water supply, and skilled scientists are on the front lines neutralizing these toxins before they can harm or kill people.

CHAPTER TWO

Reusing Wastewater

> **"**We're reaching the point where no part of the country has water to waste any longer. We know that any region is vulnerable to drought, and we know that every region is vulnerable to climate change.**"**

—Peter Gleick, cofounder of Pacific Institute, which studies water issues

Quoted in Anne C. Mulkern, "Californians Tap Technology—and Psychology—to Stretch Water Supplies," E&E News, May 12, 2016. www.eenews.net.

San Diego, California, is known for its warm days and sunny skies. But the same great weather that makes this Southern California city so attractive to tourists poses serious problems for the region's water scientists. With its semiarid climate, San Diego averages only 10 inches (25 cm) of rain per year. And in drought years—like those between 2010 and 2015—the city received much less rain.

Sixty percent of the drinking water consumed by the 3 million people living in San Diego County is piped in from the Colorado River, located about 160 miles (257 km) to the east on the Arizona-California border. Another 20 percent of San Diego water comes from rivers that originate in the Sierra Nevada, a mountain range located in California's central valley. The water travels hundreds of miles through a system of pipelines, canals, and reservoirs before it reaches residents' taps.

Both of San Diego's major water sources are threatened by overuse and climate change. City water scientists know that San Diego needs a reliable local source of water and have been working to provide one. In 2017 a high-profile $3 billion project called Pure Water San Diego was scaling up to provide a safe, sustainable, drought-proof source of water for San Diego residents. By 2023 project planners aim to produce 30 million gallons (114 million L) of drinking water every day from wastewater—the liquid mess flushed down toilets and drains.

Reusing wastewater has long been controversial, and critics call the process "toilet-to-tap."[5] This phrase captures what is called the "yuck factor"—the view that water sourced this way is somehow disgusting or contaminated. But according to San Diego water manager Brent Eidson, recycled wastewater is "completely clean. It's almost as pure as distilled water."[6]

The proper name for the toilet-to-tap method is direct potable reuse (DPR). The process cleans up the two main types of sewage generated by city residents. Gray water is the soapy wastewater from sinks, showers, dishwashers, and washing machines, and black water contains human sewage flushed down toilets. When the Pure Water project is completed, San Diego will be the first city in California to use the DPR method. It will join two other cities in Texas—Big Spring and Wichita Falls—where DPR water has been available since 2013.

Processing Effluent

Before consumers drink water produced through the DPR process, it is mixed with freshwater in municipal water treatment plants. For example, in Big Spring, Texas, water managers mix one part DPR water with four parts treated water drawn from a local reservoir. Another method for recycling wastewater is called indirect potable reuse (IPR). This water is pumped back into the environment, into groundwater or surface water sources, with the intent of adding it later to drinking water supplies. Both recycling methods use chemistry, physics, microbiology, and other sciences to create drinking water from sewage pumped into wastewater treatment plants.

The DPR and IPR processes begin with wastewater known as effluent. This term refers to liquid contaminated with soap, detergents, personal care products, human waste, and other substances that go down the drain. This wastewater is mixed in sewer systems with trash and nonpoint-source pollution from highways, farm fields, and urban areas.

Transforming Wastewater into Freshwater

The contaminated water that flows down into toilets and drains can be treated and recycled and then added to a public water supply. This is known as direct potable reuse, or DPR. During the DPR process, wastewater collected by a reclamation plant undergoes three stringent stages of purification: microfiltration, reverse osmosis, and ultraviolet disinfection. It is during these stages that all impurities, bacteria, toxins, and any other contaminants are removed—with clean, drinkable water being the end result.

Water Reclamation Plant
Collection and treatment of used water in accordance to international standards.

Freshwater
High-grade recycled water

The DPR water is blended with freshwater from natural sources and piped into the homes of consumers.

Treated Used Water

Treatment Plant

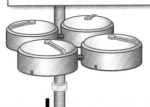

Microfiltration
Microscopic particles, including some bacteria, are filtered out in this stage.

Reverse Osmosis
Undesirable contaminants are removed here. The water after this stage is high-grade water.

Ultraviolet Disinfection
The water passes through ultraviolet light to ensure that any remaining organisms are eradicated. Chemicals are then added to restore pH balance. The water is now ready for use.

Source: PUB (Singapore's National Water Agency), "NEWater." www.pub.gov.sg.

Once the effluent enters the wastewater treatment plant, it is cleaned through a two-stage process. The first stage is called primary treatment. This stage begins when wastewater passes through a series of screens before entering the treatment plant. The screens filter out large debris and any objects that can be carried through a sewer. This material might include branches, plastic trash, clothing, dog waste, and dead animals. After the rubbish is filtered out, the wastewater is sent to a chamber, where smaller solid materials like sand and grit settle to the bottom.

Removing Biosolids

The next step in the primary treatment process is to remove bio-solids. After the wastewater is screened, it proceeds into a primary sedimentation tank for ninety minutes, during which about half of the suspensions settle out. This collection of semisolids is referred to as sewage sludge or biosolids. The material is extracted from the bottom of the sedimentation tank and passed into a sludge digestion tank, where it is digested by anaerobic bacteria. *Anaerobic* means "living without air." During anaerobic digestion, bacteria break down organic material in the absence of oxygen. When this process occurs, microbes produce bio-gas, which consist of methane, carbon dioxide, and water.

> **WORDS IN CONTEXT**
>
> **aeration**
>
> The process of introducing air into a liquid or other substance.

Scientists have devised a process in which anaerobic digestion occurs in a controlled environment called a bio-gas recovery system. The methane that is produced during the anaerobic digestion process is similar to natural gas in its chemical composition. Like natural gas, bio-gas can be used as transportation fuel or burned to generate heat or electricity.

After sewage sludge is treated by bacteria, odor-reduced solids are left behind. This material is either transported to a landfill, used on croplands as fertilizer, or bagged and marketed at garden centers as biosolid compost.

Cleaning with Microorganisms

While primary treatment relies on gravity to remove solids from wastewater, the secondary phase relies on helpful microorganisms to clean the water. Microorganisms used in wastewater treatment belong to several major groups. Bacteria feed on organic nutrients; protozoa digest algae and other suspended particles; multicellular organisms called metazoans consume fungi and microscopic creatures like roundworms.

The process begins when the partially treated wastewater flows into an aeration tank. Air bubbles are injected to add oxygen while simultaneously mixing the liquid. Certain microorganisms thrive and multiply in the oxygen-rich environment. The microbes consume

One stage of the process used to treat wastewater involves the water flowing into an aeration tank (pictured). In the tank, air bubbles are added to the water, enabling the microorganisms in the water that consume organic matter to flourish.

organic matter as food. Each individual microbe is surrounded by a cell wall that keeps the organism together. As microbes consume matter, they develop a sticky layer of slime around the outer layer of their cell wall. This layer allows them to clump together as floc.

After the aeration tank, the mixture of bacteria and wastewater flows into a settling basin called a clarifier, where most of the floc is allowed to settle to the bottom. However, some of the floc, called return activated sludge, is recycled back into the aeration tank. This ensures that adequate amounts of helpful bacteria are present as the aeration process continues.

The aeration-bacteria procedure is very efficient; it removes 85 percent to 95 percent of the solids. As wastewater scientist

BIOSOLIDS AND POLLUTION

The term *biosolids* refers to the sewage sludge left over from municipal wastewater treatment. Every year millions of tons of biosolids are recycled into fertilizer and are spread on fields where food crops are grown. But the practice is controversial; biosolids retain numerous hazardous materials, including household, medical, chemical, and industrial waste. When biosolids are used as fertilizer, traces of these toxins accumulate in the soil and are taken up by crops. Some environmental scientists believe this puts public health at risk.

There are several major categories of waste found in biosolids. Persistent organic pollutants include industrial chemicals like PCBs and dioxins. These chemicals do not biodegrade—meaning they persist in the environment. The pollutants, along with heavy metals like lead, mercury, and cadmium, pass up the food chain from plants to people. When livestock eat food grown in contaminated biosolids, the chemicals accumulate in their flesh. When people eat pork, beef, chicken, and other animals, these pollutants enter the body and can cause cancer and other disorders.

Nanoparticles are another health concern. Many consumer products such as sunscreens and cosmetics contain nanoparticles like silver or zinc oxide. These microscopic particles have a diameter of only 1 to 100 nanometers—about 1/1000 the width of a human hair. Nanoparticles pass through treatment plants and accumulate in biosolids. Like other pollutants in biosolids, nanomaterials can potentially harm people, plants, and animals.

Dan Theobald explains, "Microbiological treatment of wastewater is by far the most natural and effective process for removing wastes from water."[7] However, efficiency depends on the quality of the wastewater. Excessive quantities of soaps or detergents can produce suds and frothing that create problems for water scientists. In areas where industrial waste is part of the wastewater stream, toxic chemicals can disrupt biological activity. In such cases the water must be pretreated to remove chemicals before it moves through the activated sludge treatment process.

A Third Level of Treatment

After primary treatment, wastewater meets what EPA regulations define as sufficient cleanup standards. These standards ensure that the treated effluent will not kill fish or other marine creatures when it is returned to rivers, lakes, or other waterways. To meet sufficient cleanup standards, the water must be free of excessive nutrients like phosphorus and nitrogen, by-products of fertilizers and pet waste runoff that flow into sewers when it rains. These nutrients can cause rampant algae growth that will kill plants, fish, and other aquatic animals.

In some regions water that meets EPA standards undergoes a third cleaning in what is called a tertiary process. This phase creates what is called nonpotable, or recycled, water. Nonpotable water is used for irrigation and for business and industrial purposes such as mining and manufacturing.

The first step in tertiary treatment is called chemical coagulation. Chemicals such as alum, iron salts, and calcium carbonate (lime) are added to the water to remove tiny solids left behind by the other cleaning processes. Chemical coagulation removes 95 percent of the solids, which become heavier than water, flocculate, and settle out. Another step in the process involves filtering the water through a bed of sand to remove remaining suspended particles. Water might also contain numerous industrial chemicals

> **WORDS IN CONTEXT**
>
> **tertiary**
> Third; refers to the third level of cleaning in the DPR process.

like dyes, pesticides, and toxic waste products called halogenated hydrocarbons. These substances combine compounds made from hydrogen and carbon (hydrocarbons) with chlorine, the chemical iodine, or the corrosive elements bromine and fluorine. The deadliest forms of halogenated hydrocarbons are referred to as polychlorinated biphenyls (PCBs). These chemicals can be filtered out by passing water through a bed of activated carbon.

Nitrogen- and Phosphorus-Eating Bacteria

Effluent often contains ammonia, even after primary and secondary treatment. But ammonia can be neutralized by converting it to nitrogen in a biological process called nitrifying or nitrification. Nitrifying microorganisms called ammonia-oxidizing bacteria and ammonia-oxidizing archaea are added to the water. The microbes consume ammonia and leave nontoxic nitrate behind. However, nitrate can present another problem; because it is a nutrient, too much of the substance can cause harmful algae blooms.

In situations where nitrogen must be completely removed from the water, other types of bacteria are put to work to convert nitrates to nitrogen gas. The process is called denitrification, and it works on a molecular level. The chemical name for nitrate is NO_3; it is one nitrogen molecule surrounded by three oxygen molecules. During denitrification, effluent is pumped into a tank devoid of oxygen. In this oxygen-free environment, bacteria consume the oxygen molecules attached to the nitrate, leaving nitrogen gas behind. Nitrogen makes up almost 80 percent of the air in earth's atmosphere. The gas can be released during the denitrification process without causing harm to the environment.

Like nitrogen, phosphorus is a nutrient that contributes to algae growth. The chemical is removed during the tertiary phase in

> ### WORDS IN CONTEXT
>
> #### archaea
> Microorganisms similar to bacteria in size and simplicity but different in metabolic function.
>
> #### denitrification
> The process of removing nitrates from water, soil, or air.

THE OMNI PROCESSOR

Wastewater recycling is usually done at large municipal water plants. But the same techniques can be put to work on a much smaller scale to produce potable water for small, isolated communities. That is the thinking behind the Omni Processor designed and built in 2015 by Peter Janicki in Sedro-Woolley, Washington. The $1.5 million Omni Processor is about the size of two school buses, one stacked on top of the other. The Omni Processor simultaneously disposes of sewage, creates potable water, and generates steam-powered electricity.

The machine was designed to process 14 tons (12.7 metric tons) of sewage every day while producing enough potable water for one hundred thousand people. The sewage is fed into the machine on a conveyor belt and passes through a series of large heating tubes that boil the sludge. The boiling process creates water vapor and leaves the solids in the sewage behind. The dried solids are fed into a furnace that produces high-temperature steam. The steam drives a generator to produce electricity, which is delivered to the local community.

The water vapor created in the boiling process is condensed back into liquid and cleaned. A series of fine mesh and charcoal filters removes particles and other substances. The final product is pure, drinkable water that meets or exceeds EPA standards.

a process called enhanced biological phosphorus removal. The procedure involves bacteria called polyphosphate-accumulating organisms. These bacteria consume large amounts of phosphorus and accumulate it within their cells. When their cells are full, the polyphosphate-accumulating organisms will have a mass that is 20 percent phosphorus, which makes them highly valued as fertilizer once they are separated from the treated water.

Reverse Osmosis

After the tertiary phase, water is still not considered potable. Before it is considered clean enough to drink, the water must pass through several more steps. The first involves a microfilter known as a semipermeable membrane. A microfilter has billions of tiny holes about 1/300 the width of a human hair. The pores in the membrane are large enough to allow the passage of water molecules. Substances with larger molecules, such as oils, chemicals, and harmful bacteria, cannot pass through the filter.

For water to be of DPR quality, it must undergo a second filtering process called reverse osmosis (RO) to remove any remaining grit, impurities, salt, or other contaminants. The foundation of RO is a naturally occurring process called osmosis. The two concepts are best explained using seawater as an example. In osmosis, fluids, called solutions, flow through a semipermeable membrane. When the two solutions are freshwater and seawater, the freshwater is naturally drawn through the membrane toward the seawater because seawater is a more concentrated solution. It contains sodium and calcium ions that make it heavier and denser than freshwater. Scientists say freshwater is a weaker solution. In osmosis, a weaker solution will always flow through a semipermeable membrane toward a more concentrated solution. Osmosis occurs frequently in nature with many types of substances. A good example of osmosis is when plant roots absorb water from the soil while filtering out sand, microbes, and other unwanted elements.

RO is the osmosis process in reverse—a more concentrated solution (seawater) flows through a membrane toward a weaker solution (freshwater). With RO, the semipermeable membrane filters out the salt in seawater as the liquid flows toward freshwater. But RO is not a natural process—high-pressure electric pumps are required to push the concentrated solution through the membrane into the weaker solution. When DPR water is created, the water is pumped through the semipermeable membrane into the freshwater, and the contaminants are filtered out.

The final step is called the advanced oxidation process. During this procedure, water is exposed to ozone, which causes a chemical reaction that destroys the atoms of toxic molecules found in pesticides, petroleum products, halogenated hydrocarbons, and other pollutants. The advanced oxidation pro-

> **WORDS IN CONTEXT**
>
> ---
>
> **oxidation**
>
> A chemical process that adds oxygen to change a compound.

cess also kills bacteria and viruses and converts dissolved iron, manganese, and sulfur into solid particles that settle out of the water.

Ozone is an unstable gas composed of three oxygen atoms. It is produced in nature by the sun and by lightning. Water treatment plants produce the gas with an ozone generator that features a high-intensity ultraviolet (UV) light chamber. Oxygen is exposed to UV rays in the light chamber. This exposure causes oxygen to pick up an extra oxygen atom that is weakly attached to the other two oxygen atoms. The resulting ozone gas is bubbled through water. During the procedure, the weakly attached atom transfers itself to contaminants, causing them to oxidize. Oxidation turns the pollutants into less harmful substances, resulting in water that is as clean, or cleaner, than fresh tap water.

Another oxidation treatment method relies on a combination of UV light and hydrogen peroxide. The energy produced by the UV light breaks apart the chemical bonds of contaminants while the hydrogen peroxide oxidizes the chemicals to destroy them.

Some Impurities Remain

Despite its many cleaning stages, the DPR process is not perfect; small percentages of chemicals and impurities are left behind after the filtering and oxidation processes. Critics of the DPR water process are most concerned about traces of prescription medications. Over 60 percent of Americans consume prescription drugs like cholesterol-lowering statins, birth control pills, pain medications, and antidepressants. Almost everyone takes common pain medications like acetaminophen and ibuprofen. Small portions of these drugs pass through the human body and are flushed into the sewer system. The drugs end up in wastewater treatment plants, where they mingle with medicines taken by millions of other people. In 2013 the EPA tested clean water samples produced by fifty large wastewater treatment facilities. The agency found that half the samples contained traces of prescription drugs.

The advanced oxidation process removes 60 percent to 90 percent of the medications, but some believe this is inadequate.

More than 60 percent of Americans take prescription medications, traces of which can end up in the water supply. Researchers are studying the possibility of using a form of charcoal to strip these substances from water.

According to chemistry professor Shane Snyder, treating the water in a DPR facility might change the drugs into something even more harmful. "If you put in ozone or advance oxidization to take out a compound, when you oxidize chemicals it becomes something different. So while it's no longer a statin [drug] it's now some byproduct. It's now very common to make water more toxic after treatment than it was before treatment."[8]

In 2016 the problem of pharmaceuticals in treated water was being addressed by researcher Avni Solanki at the University of Florida. Solanki found that a cheap porous material called biochar can be used to extract drugs from wastewater. Biochar is charcoal produced by burning wood, grass, corn stalks, rice straw, fallen leaves, and other plant matter. Pharmaceutical molecules bind to biochar. Nitrogen and phosphorus, which are also present in wastewater, are left behind as by-products. These nutrients can be recycled into high-quality fertilizer. Solanki says she was excited "to see that something this cheap with such a low environmental footprint could actually be applied for pharmaceutical removal and nutrient recovery."[9] While biochar is promising, researchers have not found an effective way to incorporate it into large-scale DPR treatment plants.

An Answer to Water Scarcity

The methods used to produce DPR water have been in existence for decades. However, the public is just beginning to accept that water flushed down the toilet can be recycled back into their kitchen and bathroom faucets. But water scarcity is a national issue. According to the EPA, forty out of fifty states will face water shortages by 2025 due to extended droughts and other problems traced to climate change. And water scarcity is already a fact of life in many regions of China, India, the Middle East, and Africa. According to the United Nations, two-thirds of the world, or about 5.3 billion people, will face water shortages in the next decade. DPR will not solve all of the world's water problems, but it will play an ever-larger role in the coming years.

CHAPTER THREE

Desalination

> **"**[There's a desalination] revolution, and it's only just emerging, so we can expect a lot of technological advancements along the way to make desalination even more efficient and cost-effective.**"**

—Stanley Weiner, chief executive officer of STW Resources

Quoted in James Stafford, "The Game-Changing Water Revolution: Interview with Stanley Weiner," OilPrice.com, April 13, 2015. http://oilprice.com.

China is the world's most populous country, and it has one of the fastest-growing economies in the world. In 2015 almost half of all consumer goods in the world originated in China. All of that production requires a massive amount of freshwater. And China is facing major water shortages; in 2017 the nation was home to 21 percent of the world's population but only 7 percent of its freshwater supplies. According to China's environmental agency, 400 out of 661 cities there are facing water shortages.

Driven by this stark reality, China is embracing desalination, the process of producing freshwater from seawater. Chinese government planners hope to desalinate 807 million gallons (3.06 billion L) of seawater a day by 2020. This goal would quadruple the country's 2015 water capacity. However, desalination requires a lot of energy, and 80 percent of China's electricity is produced by coal, which contributes to pollution problems and climate change.

In 2016 China had 57 desalination projects either in progress or completed. These facilities were among the more than 18,400 desalination plants operating worldwide. Together, these facilities produced 2.9 billion gallons (11 billion L) of freshwater per day. While desalination provides water to around 300 million people in 150 nations, this is only 4 percent of all people on earth. Scientists hope to greatly expand desalination in the coming years as they conduct research into making it more economical, energy efficient, and sustainable.

Boiling Basics

The basic concept behind desalination is distillation, one of the oldest sciences known to humanity. People have been distilling water since ancient times in a process known as thermal distillation. The term *thermal* relates to heat.

China's fast-growing economy has resulted in a demand for water that the country is trying to address through desalination, the process of producing freshwater from seawater. Here, a Chinese worker monitors the production of bottled water in a desalination plant.

The science behind thermal distillation is based on the way molecules of water behave. The molecules in liquid water are attracted to each other, but they vibrate when exposed to heat. As more heat is added, the molecules vibrate faster and faster. Eventually, the liquid molecules are moving so fast that they lose their attraction to one another and begin smashing into each other like pool balls on a pool table. When the temperature of water reaches 212°F (100°C), the water begins to boil. During this process, water molecules convert from liquid to steam.

Salt boils at 2,575°F (1,413°C), a much higher temperature than water. When salt water is boiled, the bonds between salt molecules do not break apart. Mineral molecules in the water, such as magnesium and calcium, also have a high boiling point and remain stable. This higher heat threshold allows the water to evaporate first, leaving salt and minerals behind. The steam from the boiling water is collected on a condenser, and the molecules cool and then return to their liquid state. When the vibrations of the molecules slow down, they draw together like pool balls scattering in reverse, creating distilled water free of salt and mineral content.

Multistage Flash

Thermal distillation of seawater requires a substantial amount of energy; heat must be constantly applied to keep salt water boiling until it evaporates. This need for constant energy makes the process impractical for large-scale desalination. A more energy-efficient thermal distillation method is called multistage flash (MSF) distillation. It is used in about 60 percent of the world's desalination plants.

MSF distillation plants operate on the fact that water can boil without heat. Water molecules can be made to vibrate rapidly enough to turn to steam if the air pressure above the water is lowered. If water at room temperature is placed in a vacuum chamber and enough air is removed (thus lowering the air pressure), the water will boil without heating. Without the air pressure, the surface molecules of the water are no longer held in place. They vibrate so fast that they lose their connection to one another and convert to their gas state, or steam.

In an MSF distillation plant, water passes through a series of stages. Each stage has a lower water pressure than the last. The MSF process begins when seawater enters a vessel called a brine heater, where it is heated to near boiling. The heated water flows into the first stage, where the air pressure is so low the water temperature rises quickly. The escalation in temperature causes the seawater to "flash," almost exploding into steam. The steam is collected, condensed, and cooled into freshwater. Only a small percentage of the seawater is converted into steam before it cools again. The remaining seawater passes into the next stage, where the air pressure is even lower, causing the water to flash boil once again. The process is repeated, with the water being flash boiled at each stage without more heat being added. A typical MSF plant uses twenty to thirty stages to flash boil seawater. The facilities are more energy efficient than thermal distillation plants because most of the energy consumed powers the brine heater.

DEALING WITH SALTY BRINE

The brine produced by RO desalination plants is twice as salty as seawater. The substance causes problems when discharged into the ocean because waves and tides do not adequately dilute it. The high concentration of salt in brine kills most living creatures that are exposed to it. California scientists at Humboldt State University and the University of Southern California are working to solve the environmental problems associated with brine. It involves a two-step process called reverse osmosis–pressure-retarded osmosis (RO-PRO).

The RO-PRO concept is based on the idea that during osmosis, water levels rise on the side with the most concentrated solution (the salty side). If the rising salt water is in an enclosed tube, it creates pressure as it rises. This process is called pressure-retarded osmosis. The pressure can be used to spin a rotating machine called a turbine, which creates power. The power of the spinning turbine is directed to push seawater through the filter of the RO part of the system. The brine that is left behind is diverted back for use in the first step of the process, so that it is diluted by freshwater. In addition to solving the brine problem, the RO-PRO process uses 30 percent less energy than traditional RO systems.

Reverse Osmosis

Most MSF distillation facilities use technology developed in the 1950s and have changed little since that time. In the twenty-first century, almost all new desalination plants use the RO process, which is more energy efficient than the MSF process. Semipermeable membranes are made from a type of plastic called a polymer, and they are central to the RO process. Electric pumps push seawater through the membranes, which allow only water molecules

This desalination plant in Israel employs a process known as reverse osmosis. In this process, seawater is pushed through filters that remove the salt particles from it.

to pass. Larger molecules of various salts are caught in the filter. Semipermeable membranes remove up to 99 percent of the salt. The process leaves behind muck called brine that is twice as salty as seawater. A typical desalination plant creates 1 gallon (3.8 L) of brine for every gallon of freshwater produced. This waste product is discharged back into the ocean.

While RO desalination plants use less energy than MSF facilities, they still consume a lot of power. Desalination plants use from five to ten times more electricity than traditional metropolitan drinking water treatment plants. The increased use of electricity makes desalinated water about twice as expensive as conventionally treated freshwater. Since most desalination plants depend on fossil fuels for their electricity, the process contributes to air pollution and climate change. But scientists and engineers are developing solar-powered desalination plants that have less of an environmental impact.

The world's largest solar-powered RO desalination plant is being built in an unlikely place—Saudi Arabia, the world's leading oil producer. The nation currently relies on oil-fired thermal desalination plants for 70 percent of its water. Rather than burn oil to create tap water, the Saudis are harnessing the energy of the sun to power the Al Khafji desalination facility. When the plant opens in 2018, it will feature a 15-megawatt solar array that can generate the same amount of electricity as it would take to power fifteen thousand homes every day. The solar cells are polycrystalline silicon. Like all solar cells, they generate electricity by converting the

sun's electromagnetic energy, called photons, into power. When the photons strike the material in the solar cell, they are converted to electrons. These free electrons are captured, and an electrical current is generated. When the plant opens, the solar panels will power pumps and other equipment in the desalination plant designed to supply Al Khafji's one hundred thousand residents with all of their freshwater.

Forward Osmosis

In 2017 only 1 percent of the world's desalination plants were solar powered. It turns out the sun might be an impractical power source for most facilities; the solar array used in Al Khafji fills a 222-acre (90-ha) plot of land. Most desalination plants do not have that much land to spare. However, traditional desalination plants can be retrofitted with new types of filtering systems that consume much less energy.

A filtering method called forward osmosis is one way scientists hope to address the problem of high energy consumption during the desalination process. Forward osmosis is similar to RO but is more efficient. Rather than push water through a membrane at high pressure, as in RO, forward osmosis pulls seawater through a filter at low pressure. The pulling action does not require an electric pump. Forward osmosis relies on what is called a draw solution to move the water through the membrane. The draw solution is made of freshwater and a saline gas made from ammonia and carbon dioxide. The gas makes the draw solution more concentrated than seawater. Because weak solutions are always drawn toward more concentrated solutions, in forward osmosis the draw solution pulls seawater forward through the filter. A semipermeable membrane removes the salt. After the water is pulled in, it is heated enough to release the gas, which is recycled back into the process. Freshwater is left behind. Forward osmosis requires only 15 percent to 20 percent of the energy typically used in RO desalination, which lowers the cost of desalinated water significantly. In 2017 forward osmosis was only being used experimentally in desalination plants in Gibraltar and Oman, but scientists were working to develop the technology for commercial purposes in the near future.

Pervaporation

Forward osmosis might be the most energy-efficient way to desalinate water in a large facility, but the technology still requires electricity for various functions. To lower desalination costs even further, scientists are hoping to reinvent the semipermeable membrane. The next generation of filters will not need electricity to separate salt from water.

DESALINATION WITH A SOLAR STILL

In 2016 a California company called WaterFX began using a $1 million machine called a solar still to clean salt, fertilizers, and other chemicals from agricultural runoff. The solar still uses a 377-foot (115-m) array of parabolic, or curved, mirrors to capture the sun's rays. The mirrors focus the sun on tubes containing mineral oil that are suspended over the solar array. The oil warms to 248°F (120°C) and is pumped into an evaporation tank filled with salty, polluted agricultural runoff that is a by-product of irrigation. The steam produced from the heat condenses the freshwater and leaves behind the salt and chemicals. The desalinated water is as clean as bottled drinking water.

In addition to cleaning water, the solar still has numerous other benefits. The system generates excess steam that is used to power the steam pump that moves the mineral oil through the array. The chemicals left behind in the process are recycled; magnesium salts are used by the medical industry, and nitrogen is used to make gunpowder. The solar still can produce 717 million gallons (2.7 billion L) of desalinated water per year. The freshwater it produces is 75 percent cheaper than desalinated water created through conventional methods.

A team of scientists at Alexandria University in Egypt have created a very inexpensive membrane that uses cellulose acetate, a fiber derived from wood pulp. Cellulose acetate is cheap and easy to make in any laboratory. A membrane made with the material can be used to desalinate highly concentrated seawater. The filter is used in a two-step process called pervaporation. The first step involves filtering the seawater through the cellulose acetate membrane to remove salt particles. During the second step the water is exposed to a process called once-through purge-air pervaporation. During this step the water is moved to a chamber with low air pressure, causing it to vaporize. The resulting steam is collected and condensed into freshwater. Pervaporation is faster, cleaner, and more energy efficient than conventional methods, according to Alexandria University scientist Ahmed El-Shafei. He states, "Using pervaporation eliminates the need for electricity that is used in classic desalination processes, thus cutting costs significantly."[10]

Researchers are planning to adapt the pervaporation technology for commercial use by creating large sheets of cellulose acetate membrane. In 2017 the Alexandria University team established a small pervaporation desalination facility as a pilot project.

Nanotechnology

Some scientists aim to lower desalination energy consumption by incorporating cutting-edge nanotechnology into the process. Nanotechnology involves manipulating matter on an atomic or molecular level. Water scientists are focusing on tiny tubes called carbon nanotubes (CNTs). CNTs are composed of graphene, an extremely thin substance made from graphite. Under a microscope, CNTs resemble sheets of flat carbon, one atom thick, rolled into incredibly tiny tubes (like drinking straws) with a diameter of 1 to 100 nanometers—about one thousand times thinner than a human hair.

CNTs have a property that makes them especially efficient in desalination; they are hydrophobic. *Hydro* means "water" and *phobic* means "having an aversion to something." Hydrophobic molecules in CNTs repel or fail to mix with water. While using hydrophobic material to filter water does not seem to make sense, CNTs can be modified to take advantage of their water-aversion quality.

The top of each CNT is coated with molecules that attract seawater to the opening. In scientific terms, the tubes are tip functionalized. The molecules are referred to as zwitterion—each molecule has both a positive and negative electrical charge that attracts water molecules. The zwitterion molecules act as gatekeepers at the entrance of nanotubes. Their electrical charge pulls seawater into the nanotube, where the hy-

WORDS IN CONTEXT

hydrophobic
Pertaining to a substance such as oil that is adverse to, or fails to mix with, water.

zwitterion
A type of molecule with both a positive and negative electrical charge.

drophobic qualities of the CNT rapidly push the water through. The water travels one hundred times faster through a CNT than any other pore of a similar size. While zwitterion molecules attract water, the electrical charge rejects salt and pollutants in the water. This means that seawater that enters a tip-functionalized CNT exits as freshwater. And because water travels so easily through CNTs, the process requires very little energy.

While membranes made of CNTs hold promise, they are costly to produce, especially on a scale large enough for use in commercial desalination plants. But CNTs hold promise for use in small-scale applications. Researchers are looking for ways to incorporate CNT membranes into a thin fiber cloth. This material could be used by individuals in developing nations who would place the filter over water pitchers to create freshwater where it is scarce.

Living Water Channels

Another desalination method that uses electrical charges on an atomic level is modeled on living cells. Aquaporins are proteins that form tiny pores in the membranes of biological cells. Also known as water channels, they efficiently transport water in a variety of bacteria, animal, and plant cells.

Water moves in and out of most cells by osmosis through cell membranes. However, epithelial cells, which line the surfaces of blood vessels, organs, and muscle tissue, move water faster than other cells. In 2003 American molecular biologist Peter Agre won the Nobel Prize in Chemistry for discovering aquaporin water channels in this type of cell. Agre explained the discovery: "[Aquaporins are] the plumbing system for cells. Every cell is primarily water. But the water doesn't just sit in the cell, it moves through it in a very organized way. The process occurs rapidly in tissues that have these aquaporins or water channels."[11]

An aquaporin is only a few nanometers wide. It has a positive electrical charge at the center, which pulls in water while repelling salt. In 2015 a team of chemists and biomolecular scientists at the National University of Singapore incorporated aquaporins into a seawater-filtering structure called a biomimetic membrane. The membrane mimics the structure of living cells found in the roots of mangrove trees. Mangroves grow in sand and mud on seashores and in saltwater marshes. While salt water will kill most plants, mangrove roots have adapted to extract freshwater from seawater. The roots filter out 95 percent of the salt.

Mangrove trees (pictured) are able to live along seashores and in saltwater marshes because their roots filter 95 percent of salt out of the water. Scientists have developed a water-filtering structure that mimics the structure of cells in the roots.

The National University of Singapore researchers were the first in the world to succeed in bonding aquaporin proteins to a membrane. The aquaporins act as tunnels through which water can be transported. The biometric membrane is strong and stable, and in 2017 the researchers were working to incorporate it into a pilot desalination project. If the membrane can be scaled up to work in an industrial desalination plant in the future, it could provide a greater supply of drinking water at a much lower cost than methods currently available.

WORDS IN CONTEXT

biomimetic

Pertaining to synthetic methods that mimic biochemical processes.

Tiny Solutions to Large Problems

In the hands of scientists, tiny things can solve large problems. The plumbing systems of single cells might someday convert the waters of the wide ocean into glasses of drinking water. The powers of microscopic nanotubes could funnel freshwater into millions of faucets. And research into membranes, gases, and air pressure might hold the key to solving humanity's future water shortages. The concepts behind distillation and desalination are basic, but the science is becoming increasingly complex as the demand for freshwater continues to grow throughout the world.

CHAPTER FOUR

Cleaning Up Polluted Water

> "Nanoparticles will clean up the water, and you can collect them, and add [them] to another batch of polluted water and do it over again."
>
> —Tim Leshuk, nanotechnologist
>
> Quoted in Vanessa Lu, "Researchers Developing Nanoparticles to Purify Water," *Toronto Star*, January 14, 2017. www.thestar.com.

Industrial pollution is one of the major threats to freshwater resources throughout the world. Factories that produce paints, pesticides, petroleum, and plastics produce toxic chemicals and heavy metals that are dumped into waterways legally, illegally, or accidentally. According to the environmental group Nature Conservancy, 40 percent of rivers and lakes in the United States are too polluted for swimming or fishing. Worldwide, over 50 percent of the earth's groundwater is not potable, according to the United Nations. In developing countries, 70 percent of industrial waste is dumped untreated into lakes and rivers.

Once freshwater is contaminated with industrial pollution, it is extremely difficult, expensive, and sometimes impossible to remove. Some toxic chemicals break down or are diluted quickly, while others are highly persistent and remain in the environment for decades. This poses numerous challenges to scientists, who are searching for new ways to clean up pollution by using everything from native plants to nanotechnology. Whatever the problem, the goal remains the same: to make freshwater sustainable by removing harmful substances that factories flush into rivers, lakes, and aquifers.

Plants Clean Up Pollution

Polluted water cannot be used for drinking, washing, or agriculture, but scientists are learning that many contaminants can be neutralized or eliminated by working with nature. Foul water can be made potable by mimicking biological processes found in marshes, swamps, sloughs, bogs, bayous, and other saturated areas known as wetlands.

Wetlands can be found in all climates nearly everywhere in the world. They might contain water that is fresh, salty, or brackish (slightly salty). Wetlands act like strainers that filter out harmful substances. They are particularly helpful for cleaning up pollution because they are most often located between land and rivers, lakes, and oceans. When it rains, wetlands intercept nonpoint-source pollution before it enters open waters.

> **WORDS IN CONTEXT**
>
> **brackish**
>
> Pertaining to water that is a mixture of freshwater and salt water.

The term *remediation* is used by scientists when discussing the removal of pollution from the environment; remedies are selected, and remedial actions are taken to clean up water or land. *Phyto* is a prefix meaning "plants." Using plants to purify water is called phytoremediation. It is a tongue-twisting term that encompasses the cutting-edge science of pollution cleanup through natural forces. Scientists can use various techniques to either improve the filtering qualities of natural wetlands or construct wetlands to remove a specific type of pollution. But the possibilities of phytoremediation are just beginning to be understood.

Phytoremediation is based on the well-known concept that wetlands are nature's water purifiers. As water moves through wetlands, it flows past plants, submerged branches, rocks, and other debris. These objects consume or filter out bacteria and common water pollutants. Pollution also gets trapped in mud and muck. The water that flows out of wetlands is much cleaner than the water that flowed in. According to studies by the Union of Concerned Scientists, wetlands can remove 20 percent to 60 percent of heavy metals in the water and eliminate 70 percent to 90 percent of nitrogen from fertilizers, pollution, and other sources.

Oxygen Free and Water Loving

Wetlands are formed when precipitation, surface water, and groundwater flow through basins where the soil is anaerobic, or without oxygen. (This soil differs from soil elsewhere, which is aerobic—the soil contains oxygen needed by microorganisms, insects, and plant roots.) The oxygen-free soil of a wetland creates a distinct ecosystem in which anaerobic bacteria can thrive in the muck and the mud. The term *anaerobic* is somewhat misleading. These microbes do not live without oxygen but instead have evolved to obtain oxygen from nitrates. The bacteria consume oxygen from the nitrates in the water and release nitrogen gas into the atmosphere. This denitrification process cleans the water of naturally occurring nitrates and those introduced into the ecosystem from agricultural and industrial sources.

Wetland plants also have unique characteristics that allow them to remove nitrogen from the water. Many plants found in wetlands are hydrophytes, or water plants; they grow only in water. Like anaerobic bacteria, the plants have adapted to wetland conditions by developing unique features to collect oxygen. While land plants are aerobic because their roots obtain oxygen from small pockets of air in the soil, the roots of hydrophytes are submerged in the anaerobic soil underwater, so they cannot obtain oxygen this way. Instead, the hollow stems of the plants take oxygen from the air and deliver it to the roots. Species of bulrush, sedge, reed, and cattail have passageways for this purpose.

The roots of hydrophytes can absorb and transform numerous substances, including toxic hydrocarbons. These highly poisonous compounds consist of hydrogen and carbon. Toxic hydrocarbon pollution includes PCBs used in hydraulic fluids, sealants, synthetic rubber, and paint. Depending on the plant, hydrophytes can store the pollutants in the stems and leaves without hurting the plants or transform the pollutants into less harmful substances.

How Wetlands Remove Pollutants from Water

Wetlands act as nature's water purifier with mud, plants, and submerged debris consuming or removing nitrates, phosphate, and other pollutants through roots, leaves, and bacteria. The roots of the cattail (left) absorb phosphorus and use it for growth in the spring and summer. When the plant dies in the fall it decomposes into litterfall where the phosphorus is locked up in the wetland soil. The broadleaf arrowhead (right) absorbs nitrogen through its roots and stems. The plant converts nitrogen to harmless nitrogen gas (N_2) which is released into the atmosphere. Anaerobic bacteria submerged in the soil (bottom right) also consume nitrogen and release nitrogen gas.

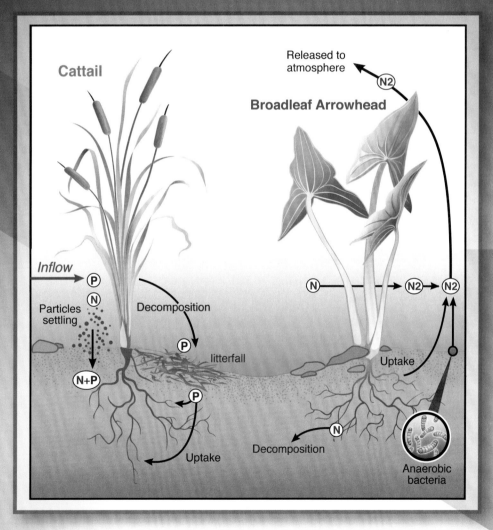

Source: The Wetlands Initiative, "Nutrient Removal." www.wetlands-initiative.org.

Myriad-Leaf in Russia

While wetlands offer an anaerobic environment, phytoremediation can also take place in aerobic conditions. This process happens in wastewater treatment plants, where oxygen is injected into effluent to stimulate aerobic microorganisms. In Russia scientists of a project funded by the Alcoa Foundation Advancing Sustainability Research program discovered that an aquatic plant called myriad-leaf improves the efficiency of pollution cleanup in an aerobic environment.

Myriad-leaf is common throughout Russia. The plant is cheap, organic, and effective in removing nitrates and phosphates from water that carries sewage and fertilizers. In 2013 researchers from Samara State Technical University planted myriad-leaf in stagnant or low-flowing bodies of water, where fertilizers caused an overgrowth of algae. The algae-created dead zones had little oxygen or aquatic life. Scientists installed large electric pumps in these ponds to oxygenate the water by aerating it. While the aeration helped clean the pond by allowing aerobic bacteria to thrive, the addition of the myriad-leaf made the process faster and more efficient.

Myriad-leaf is also being used to remediate iron and other heavy metals like hexavalent chromium, a highly reactive form of chromium, which is used in leather tanning, wood preservation, and the production of stainless steel and textile dyes. Heavy metals are particularly dangerous in freshwater because they bioaccumulate, meaning the substances build up in the bodies of living organisms and are transferred to other creatures through the food chain. For example, small fish absorb heavy metals in their liver, gills, and muscles from food, water, and sediment. These fish are eaten by bigger fish, which accumulate greater amounts of metal. If humans eat the fish, they can experience adverse health effects, in-

HOW PLANTS CLEAN WATER

When wetland plants are used to clean up pollution in the phytoremediation process, they respond to harmful substances in a variety of ways. Scientists use specific terms, listed below, to identify various methods plants use to clean up toxins.

In phytoextraction, the leaves and roots of the plant withdraw, or extract, heavy metals such as cadmium, cobalt, nickel, mercury, lead, selenium, and zinc. The leaves and roots are then harvested to remove the metals from the ecosystem.

Rhizo is a prefix meaning "root." In the rhizofiltration process, plant roots are used to absorb and concentrate heavy metals, radioactive materials, and toxic phenol-based compounds like bisphenol A, used to make plastic. Rhizofiltration is used where factory or waste facilities discharge contaminated liquid effluent.

Phytostimulation is a process in which the roots of specific types of plants stimulate the growth of helpful bacteria and fungi capable of biodegrading petroleum hydrocarbons like benzene and toluene.

Phytovolatilization is a process in which plants take up certain heavy metals like mercury and chlorine-based solvents and modify them on a molecular level. The toxicity is greatly reduced, and the by-products are safe enough to release into the atmosphere as vapor.

During the phytodecomposition process, plants capture compounds like TNT, chlorinated solvents, pesticides, and phenols. The substances are stored in the plants, which eventually die and decompose. This process transforms the compounds into less toxic or nontoxic by-products.

cluding severe damage to the liver, kidneys, and heart. Myriad-leaf can help stop this problem; studies show that when it is planted in polluted water, it can remove 75 percent of the iron. When studies were conducted with hexavalent chromium, researchers found that myriad-leaf boosted the cleaning efficiency by 50 percent within eighteen hours of contact between myriad-leaf and the metal.

Rafts of Vegetation

While Russian researchers work to clean up industrial pollution, an American inventor has created a way to remove excess nitrate and phosphate from lakes, rivers, and wetlands. The idea came

Bruce Kania stands atop one of his floating islands constructed of wetland plants and soil placed on top of plastic mesh. The plant roots grow through the raft's porous material and descend into the water below, absorbing pollutants.

to Bruce Kania in 2005 when he was canoeing on the 6.5-acre (2.6-ha) Fish Fry Lake, 30 miles (48 km) north of Billings, Montana. The lake was a dead zone due to algae blooms that thrived on fertilizer runoff from local farms. According to Kania, "Fish Fry Lake was a nutrient-rich, pea-soup green mosquito factory. You would not let your dog drink from the edge. The place stank, and when our black dog did decide to cool off and take a dip, within minutes of coming out of the water his coat would take on a reddish hue from the cyanobacteria . . . which can poison water."[12]

When Kania first canoed on the lake, he felt helpless; he could not stop local farmers from using fertilizer. Then he remembered how he paddled his canoe on pristine lakes when he was growing up in northern Wisconsin. The Wisconsin lakes contained peat mats—thin, flat, loosely consolidated mats of brown soil and vegetation such as water lilies, rushes, bladderworts, and grasses. The peat mats floated along the calm edges of lakes and in slow-moving streams, where the vegetation and bacteria helped purify the water. The peat mats can support a lot of weight, and locals call them quaking bogs because they bounce up and down when people walk on them. In addition to keeping the waters crystal clear, the peat mats provide habitat to numerous fish species and aquatic birds.

The peat mats inspired Kania to found Floating Island International in 2005. He assembled a team of scientists and engineers to build floating islands that would mimic the cleansing power of the peat mats of Wisconsin. He called them BioHaven floating islands. The islands are formed from layers of mesh made from recycled plastic drinking bottles. The mesh is strong enough to support the weight of wetland plants and soil, which are placed on top of the mesh. The floating rafts can be as small as a home aquarium or nearly as large as a football field. They can be anchored in place in lakes, ponds, streams, sewage lagoons, and storm water runoff ponds. Over time, the plant roots grow through the raft's porous material and descend into the water below, absorbing nitrogen and phosphorus.

The recycled mesh of the raft also provides a beneficial environment for bacteria, which colonize the floating islands. The bacteria form sticky sheets called biofilm that coat the floating matrix and the suspended plant roots. The biofilm attracts even more nitrogen and phosphorus than the plant roots, converting them into less harmful substances. As Kania explains: "The sticky biofilm essentially keeps the water clear because all the suspended solids tend to bond to it."[13]

In 2005 Kania covered about 2 percent of the surface of Fish Fry Lake with BioHaven islands. Within four years the islands had reduced the nitrogen content in the lake by 95 percent. Phosphorus concentrations dropped by nearly 40 percent. Levels of oxygen in the lake were sixty times what they once were. By 2016 Fish Fry Lake was one of the most productive fisheries in Montana, with thriving populations of black crappie, yellow perch, and cutthroat trout. The islands also provide habitat for birds, while the organic debris that attaches to the underside provides a source of food for fish and other aquatic organisms. Fish Fry Lake was thriving, as Kania explains: "The concept of how to get back to a healthy waterway is very simple: nature's wetland effect."[14] By 2016 over seven thousand BioHaven islands were in place in the United States, Canada, Australia, New Zealand, the United Kingdom, Singapore, Korea, and elsewhere.

High-Tech "Smart" Remediation

BioHaven islands perform their cleanup work over a timescale measured in months and years. But if the work of Diana Vilela can be perfected, high-tech miniature robots (microbots) will be cleaning tons of heavy metals from polluted waterways in a matter of hours. Vilela is a nanotechnology researcher developing tiny tube-shaped microbots, each one thinner than a human hair. According to Vilela, hundreds of thousands of these microbots can be deployed at once in contaminated waterways, where they can remove up to 95 percent of the lead in one hour.

The microbots have three layers that allow them to process pollution. The outer layer is made of graphene oxide, a substance that absorbs lead. The chemical name for graphene oxide, GOx, gives the tiny machines their name—GOx-microbots. The middle layer of the microbots is nickel, which makes them magnetic. This feature means the direction and motion of the microbots can be controlled by a magnetic field projected from a handheld device.

The microbot propulsion system consists of an inner layer of platinum, which uses hydrogen peroxide as fuel. When the cleaning process is initiated, researchers dump hydrogen peroxide into wastewater. The hydrogen peroxide reacts with the platinum to form water and oxygen microbubbles. The bubbles are ejected out of the microbots, and they are propelled forward.

After the microbots have finished cleaning the water, the lead ions can be cleaned off the outer layer and reused. Samuel Sánchez, who worked on the project with Vilela, explains the importance of pollution-cleaning microbots: "This work is a step toward the development of a smart remediation system where we can target and remove traces of pollutants without producing any additional contamination."[15] Researchers are hoping to develop techniques to mass-produce the GOx-microbots while improving their ability to clean up other types of pollution.

Melamine Sponges Clean Up Oil

Microbots cannot clean up oil and other petroleum-based industrial solvents, because the substances are too viscous, or sticky. But nanotechnology is providing another solution to oil cleanup: melamine sponges coated with nanoparticles. Melamine is an extremely low-weight porous material that is widely used in sponges, cleaning products, and insulation. Researchers at the Birck Nanotechnology Center at Purdue University in Indiana

NANOTECH LILY PADS

Lily pads are one of the most commonly recognized wetland plants. They root in the soil beneath the water, while their leaves and beautiful flowers float on the surface. Like many other wetland plants, lily pads clean the water by absorbing pollution. In 2014 nanotech researcher Mark Owen was inspired to create synthetic LilyPad water purifiers. The pads are about 3 feet (91 cm) in diameter and made of a plastic mesh with a coating of titanium dioxide nanoparticles. The LilyPads are solar activated; when sunlight hits the titanium dioxide, it triggers a chemical reaction that breaks down heavy metals and harmful bacteria like E. coli and salmonella. The LilyPads are simply anchored in a river, pond, or lake for months at a time. They clean the water as it flows past.

Owen used the same technology to provide clean water on a smaller scale. His company, Puralytics, manufactures a portable drinking water purifier called the SolarBag. The bag, sold in sixty countries, purifies 3.2 quarts (3 L) of water at a time. The bags utilize the titanium dioxide nanoparticles and plastic mesh found on the LilyPad. SolarBags cost under forty dollars and are being distributed by aid agencies in developing countries to provide clean drinking water to people in need. The bags are also popular with backpackers and campers.

created an oil-cleanup product by dipping melamine sponges in a solution called polydimethylsiloxane (PDMS), which is made from silicon rubber. This nanoparticle solution forms a very thin layer on the sponge that repels water while allowing the sponge to absorb oil.

In technical terms, PDMS is superhydrophobic—it strongly resists water. PDMS is also superoleophilic—it robustly attracts oil. Because melamine is very porous, it can absorb up to seventy-five times its own weight in oil and other common pollutants such as

Oil spillage can do great harm to the environment. Scientists are working on a way to clean up such spills with reusable sponges dipped in a solution that repels water and attracts oil.

engine coolant and PCBs. The sponges can be wrung out into containers specially made to handle hazardous waste. And the inexpensive sponges can be reused dozens of times, making them much cheaper than microbots. Xuemei Chen is the lead researcher on the project at the Birck Nanotechnology Center. She describes the advantages of melamine sponges coated with nanoparticles: "Oil spillage from industrial sources has caused severe damage to the environment. The conventional methods used to clean up oils and organic pollutants are slow and energy-intensive. The development of absorbent materials with high selectivity for oils is of great ecological importance for removing pollutants from contaminated water sources."[16]

Sun-Powered Nanoparticles

Nanotechnology can be used to clean up industrial pollution, and when combined with the power of the sun, nanoparticles can be used to destroy biological contamination. Scientists know that solar rays can purify water and that invisible UV rays emitted by the sun destroy germs. This is why wastewater treatment plants expose water to UV light during the purification process. In developing countries, people leave plastic bottles of water in the sun to purify the water. However, under natural conditions the process can take up to forty-eight hours because only 4 percent of solar energy is in the form of invisible UV rays. The visible part of the solar spectrum holds about 50 percent of the sun's energy. In 2016 this scientific fact inspired nanotech researchers at Stanford University to create a water purification device that utilizes visible solar rays rather than UV rays. The researchers created a tiny nanostructured device, half the size of a postage stamp, that can kill 99.99 percent of bacteria in polluted water in twenty minutes.

The unnamed device looks like a rectangle of black glass. According to lead researcher Chong Liu, "We just dropped it into the water and put everything under the Sun, and the Sun did all the work."[17] The device is coated with nanoparticles of molybdenum disulfide, a chemical composed of molybdenum and sulfur that is commonly used as an industrial lubricant.

Like many chemicals, molybdenum disulfide takes on different properties when it is reduced to nanoparticles only a few atoms thick. When molybdenum disulfide nanoparticles are exposed to sunlight and water, the nanoparticles create hydrogen peroxide to kill germs.

Viewed under an electron microscope, the material looks like a fingerprint with many closely spaced lines. These lines are atom-thick films of molybdenum disulfide called nanoflakes. When these nanoflakes are hit by sunlight, the electrons in the chemical leave their usual places and react with a copper layer that is part of the device. This reaction triggers the production of hydrogen peroxide.

While the science is complex, the results are amazing. As Liu says: "It's very exciting to see that by just designing a material you can achieve a good performance. It really works. Our intention is to solve environmental pollution problems so people can live better."[18] Molybdenum disulfide is cheap to produce, and researchers hope the device will be ready for public use by 2018. If the device can be produced on a large scale, it could make bacteria-free water available to 663 million people throughout the world who live without safe drinking water.

Contamination in freshwater can come from many sources. But advances in microbots, nanotechnology, and aquatic sustainability have shown that natural forces and technology can work together to drastically reduce the pollution found in wetlands, rivers, and lakes.

CHAPTER FIVE

Sustainable Water in Cities

> **"We have to find new ways to live that can provide good [water], comfort, productivity, and satisfaction without negative [environmental] consequences. That quest naturally starts with cities, where more than half of all people (and 80 percent of Americans) already live."**
>
> —Denis Hayes, engineer and environmentalist
>
> Denis Hayes, "Better, Faster, More," Bullitt Center, 2013. www.bullittcenter.org.

On the scale of human history, city living is a new concept. For countless centuries people lived in rural areas, where they obtained water directly from rivers, lakes, wells, and springs. Even at the beginning of the twentieth century, only 14 percent of people lived in cities. But urban growth has exploded since that time. In 2008, for the first time, over half the people on earth lived in cities, according to the United Nations. And the percentage of urban dwellers was even greater in industrialized nations. In the United States 80 percent of the population lives in cities. But as engineer and ecologist Denis Hayes points out, "The world has no sustainable cities today."[19]

Cities cannot survive without sustainable sources of freshwater. This explains why scientists, architects, and engineers are working to improve systems for drinking water, wastewater, and storm water. Some are designing more efficient ways to capture storm water. Others are working on sustainable buildings that can operate off the grid—meaning independently of a city's water, sewer, and power systems. This work is cutting edge; most city planners do not encourage builders to consider sustainability on new projects. As Hayes says: "[There are] no more than a handful of truly sustainable buildings—buildings that will still make sense 25 years from now."[20] But numerous cities throughout the world are facing critical water shortages in the twenty-first century. Billions of people are depending on new construction technologies to ensure a sustainable supply of freshwater in the future.

Precious Rainwater

California has long been considered a "green" state with strong environmental policies that promote the wise use of water. But the years from 2011 to 2016 were among the driest in California history and posed a powerful challenge to state residents. During the five-year drought, California reservoirs, which provide drinking water for most of the state's 39 million people, reached record low levels. There were fears that some cities, including Bakersfield, Santa Cruz, and Fresno, would completely run out of water. Trees died, lawns turned brown, and people took shorter showers and stopped flushing their toilets after every use.

When the drought situation in California could not have been worse, the weather changed dramatically. In early January 2017 a large, slow-moving storm that originated near Hawaii, called a Pineapple Express, took aim at California. The storm dumped heavy rain and snow throughout the state. For the next several months, powerful Pineapple Express storms, technically known as atmospheric rivers, kept coming. By April California's record-breaking drought was declared to be over.

The drought-busting rainstorms were welcome throughout the state. But in heavily populated Los Angeles they also exposed major flaws in the way the city deals with storm water. Whenever it rains in Los Angeles, billions of gallons of precious rainwater cascade off roofs and cars. The pure water washes across streets and sidewalks, runs down gutters into a maze of storm drains, and funnels into the concrete channel known as the Los Angeles River. During some storms the river water flows into

Drivers struggle through flooded streets in Los Angeles. Runoff from rainstorms in the city flows into the Pacific Ocean instead of being stored—a situation critics say needs to change in the drought-prone region.

the Pacific Ocean at a rate of 29 million gallons (110 million L) a minute. Amid one storm, Deborah Weinstein Bloome of the environmental group TreePeople watched all that freshwater dumping into Pacific. "It kills me when I see all that water running off. [It's a loss of] free liquid gold,"[21] she says.

Scientists are searching for new ways to capture and reuse rainwater to ensure a sustainable supply of freshwater in Los Angeles and elsewhere. They are also studying water-saving measures that involve urban design. Biologists, architects, and engineers are working to create structures that capture rainwater and recycle and reuse wastewater on-site. Reducing waste that flows into treatment plants is another way to save freshwater in urban regions. These efforts are critical; scientists agree that despite the record-breaking storms of 2017, long-term droughts will be common in California well into the next century due to climate change.

Capturing Runoff

When it rains in natural areas, about 30 percent of the precipitation reaches shallow aquifers that feed plants. Another 30 percent percolates into deep aquifers, where it is stored. During this process the water is cleaned as it passes through layers of dirt, sand, gravel, and bacteria that live in the soil. The remaining 40 percent of precipitation slowly evaporates into the atmosphere, where it eventually falls back to earth as rain.

These natural processes are disturbed in cities, which consist of hundreds of square miles of what urban planners call hardscape: roofs, concrete and asphalt roads, parking lots, and highways. Hardscape is referred to as an impervious surface, meaning fluids—including rain and melting snow—cannot pass through it. Water rushes down streets, picking up trash, oil, animal waste, and other contaminants as it flows into sewers. In a typical city only 5 percent of precipitation makes its way into deep aquifers, while 15 percent evaporates. About 75 percent of rainwater becomes surface runoff.

Los Angeles provides an example of how the hardscape wastes rainwater. The Pineapple Express storms that hit Los Angeles during the last two weeks of January 2017 dumped an estimated 25 billion gallons (94.6 billion L) of storm water on the city—an amount equal to 14 percent of all the water city residents use in an average year. About 2 billion gallons (7.6 billion L) of that water percolated through the soil in yards, parks, golf courses, and other unpaved areas. This water also flowed into the Los Angeles aquifer, which provides the city with about 12 percent of its water. Another 2 billion gallons (7.6 billion L) from the January storms was captured behind dams or in small collec-

PERMEABLE PAVING

In many large cities more than half the land is covered with buildings, roads, sidewalks, and parking lots. All of these materials and structures prevent precipitation from entering the soil and passing into aquifers. Scientists and engineers are beginning to address this problem with permeable paving, porous materials that allow storm water to pass into the soil.

The term *permeable paving* can refer to either pervious concrete or porous asphalt. Pervious concrete is made with carefully controlled amounts of water and cement that are used to coat pieces of crushed stone or gravel called aggregate. Unlike regular concrete, the substance contains no sand, which would make the material impervious. Roads made with this cement-coated gravel are highly porous.

Porous asphalt is based on the black, oil-based substance commonly used on roads and parking lots. Porous asphalt consists of rocks glued together with asphalt. As with pervious concrete, sand is not added, leaving open spaces in the material that allow water to flow through.

Permeable roadways consist of several layers. The bottom is made up of a permeable material called geotextile fabric that lies on the soil. This material allows water to pass but traps pollutants to ensure contamination does not enter the groundwater. Several layers of crushed gravel of various sizes are laid above the fabric. A 5-inch (13-cm) layer of porous asphalt or pervious concrete completes the roadway. After installation is complete rainwater can penetrate the roadway and filter into the aquifer below.

tion ponds called spreading grounds. The other 21 billion gallons (79.5 billion L) of water flowed out to sea.

While no municipal storm water system could capture all of the rain produced by a Pineapple Express, Los Angeles is hoping to do better. As David Pettijohn, water resources director for the Los Angeles Department of Water and Power, points out, streets cannot be torn up to allow water to pass. "So what do you do? You build stormwater capture projects that get water back into the ground,"[22] he says.

Los Angeles took a major step toward getting the water back in the ground with the construction of the Tujunga Spreading Grounds, to be completed in 2018. This 150-acre (61-ha) tract of porous soil lies in the San Fernando Valley, north of downtown Los Angeles. The spreading grounds are located over known aquifers and are designed to capture storm water that runs off from mountains and hills that surround the Los Angeles Basin. The project is expected to annually recharge the aquifer known as the San Fernando Groundwater Basin with 5 billion gallons (19 billion L) of water—enough for forty-eight thousand households.

The Ultimate Net Zero Water Building

While cities struggle to build larger water reserves, environmental scientists, architects, and engineers are using next-generation building systems to create structures that are not dependent on municipal water systems. One of the best examples is a Seattle, Washington, office building called the Bullitt Center, completed in 2013. The six-story Bullitt Center bills itself as the greenest commercial building in the world. It is powered by a solar array on the roof. The Bullitt Center is also a net zero water building. A building with this designation contains systems that harvest rainwater, recycle wastewater, and use water-efficient appliances.

The water and sewage processing systems of the Bullitt Center are self-contained; the building is not connected to Seattle's municipal water supply or its wastewater disposal system. All drinking water used in the Bullitt Center comes from rainwater collected on-site. The building's roof is surrounded by a wall that creates a shallow pool to collect precipitation when it rains. Downspouts take the water to a 56,000-gallon (211,983-L) concrete cistern, or storage tank, located in the office building's basement. The tank holds a 104-day supply of water, enough to take care of the tenants' needs throughout the dry summer months.

Before the rainwater reaches the cistern, it travels through a debris screen to remove large particles. The rainwater is then purified on-site. The rainwater is finely filtered as it passes through three microfilters. The smallest mesh size is 0.2 microns (a human hair is about 45 microns). The filters are ceramic and made of a porous clay-based material similar to that used in earthenware pots. As the water seeps through the millions of pores in the ceramic material, viruses and contaminants are filtered out. The rainwater also flows past a UV light and through activated charcoal at a speed of 5 gallons (19 L) per minute. The water

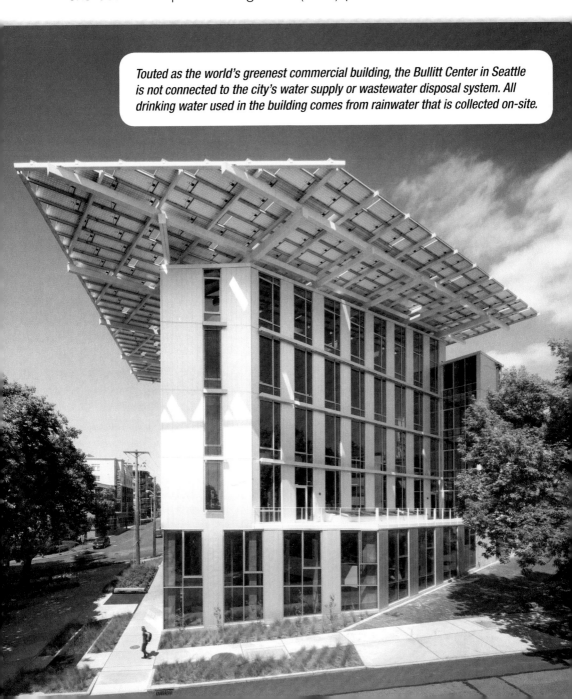

Touted as the world's greenest commercial building, the Bullitt Center in Seattle is not connected to the city's water supply or wastewater disposal system. All drinking water used in the building comes from rainwater that is collected on-site.

is clean enough to drink, but a small amount of chlorine must be added to satisfy city drinking water regulations. The filtered water is stored in a 500-gallon (1,893-L) tank that is connected to drinking water spigots throughout the building. Bullitt Center spokesperson Brad Kahn believes that self-contained drinking water systems will become more necessary in the future as the effects of climate change increase the chances of drought even in rainy cities like Seattle. "We're doing this because some day, as a region, we'll have to think about where our water comes from," says Kahn. "That day is getting closer. We wanted to drive that conversation."[23]

Wastewater Reuse

The net zero water system in the Bullitt Center is also built with different equipment to handle gray water and black water. (Cities' wastewater treatment systems do not separate gray water from black water.) Gray water treatment at the Bullitt Center depends on residents using biodegradable soap that can be decomposed naturally by bacteria and other living organisms. When residents create gray water, it drains into a 500-gallon (1,893-L) storage tank before being pumped into a constructed wetland on the building's third floor.

The Bullitt Center wetland mimics the functions of a marsh in nature. It contains layers of porous gravel and soil, where wetland plants known as horsetails are grown. The gray water is slowly pumped through a series of drip lines that allow the horsetail roots to absorb the nutrients in the water. After the water makes a pass through the wetland, it is collected and pumped through the system several more times. It is finally released into a gently curved concrete landscape element called a bioswale located next to the building. The 20-foot-long (6-m) structure is constructed with gently sloped sides and is filled with gravel. As water slowly flows through the bioswale, pollutants and pathogens are trapped and broken down. The water flowing out of the bioswale enters a small settling ground, where it can percolate back into the soil.

A bioswale like the gravel along this road is a structure that collects rainwater to allow it to seep back into the ground rather than flow into a sewer system. The bioswale pictured here is in New York City.

Decomposing Matter

The most complicated wastewater treatment facility in the Bullitt Center is reserved for black water. It is treated by what the Bullitt Center calls the world's only six-story composting toilet system. The system mimics nature by utilizing aerobic bacteria to break down human waste into organic compost.

The process of turning black water into fertile soil begins in the Bullitt Center's waterless toilets. These vessels are odorless; they utilize small electric fans to circulate air downward through the chamber to prevent smells from rising into the air. The toilets are not completely waterless; when they are flushed the waste is mixed with 1 cup (237 ml) of water containing 1 tablespoon (14.8 ml) of biodegradable soap. (A standard toilet uses 1.5 to 3.5 gallons [5.7 to 13.2 L] of water per flush.) This foamy mixture helps the waste slide down through vertical pipes into a basement composting system that consists of ten large blue bins. Each bin is about the size of a subcompact car—84 inches tall, 40 inches wide, and 61 inches deep (213 by 102 by 155 cm). Wood chips are blended with the liquid and solid waste. Each bin contains comblike tines that are occasionally rotated with a hand crank. The Bullitt Center website provides scientific details about the compost system:

> As the matter decomposes, the particles become smaller and smaller, and naturally filter down towards the bottom of the pile. Successful compost requires oxygen to keep the pile from going septic, or turning anaerobic. The required air is actually drawn through the toilets themselves then down the waterless pipes. To make sure that oxygen is permeating the pile, the amount of liquid is carefully managed, and spread evenly among the piles. . . . This keeps the decomposition process strictly aerobic, eliminating the release of methane gas and dangerous odors, byproducts of typical waste treatment.[24]

The system generates biosolids and liquid waste called leachate. The leachate is pumped out once a month and transported to a county wastewater treatment plant. The biosolids are mixed with sawdust and sold as fertilizer. Several times a year the Bullitt Center six-story toilet system produces a load of rich compost prized by organic farmers for use as a fertilizer and soil conditioner. The natural acids in compost also make it valuable as a natural pesticide.

The Living Machine

The Bullitt Center is considered a Living Building, as certified by the International Living Future Institute in Seattle. Living buildings must have net zero water and net zero energy consumption. A similar building was constructed in 2012 for the San Francisco Public Utilities Commission (SFPUC), the government agency that provides San Francisco with its water. Like the Bullitt Center, the

San Francisco building harvests rainwater for drinking and generates power using a system of solar panels. But the San Francisco building wastewater treatment system is different. Rather than mimicking a freshwater wetland, the SFPUC wastewater processing plant is based on a natural tidal marsh like those found near the ocean. Tidal marshes are low-lying coastal ecosystems where water levels are constantly changing with the tides. The rising and falling action helps improve water quality by increasing oxygen levels, trapping sediment in gravel, reducing turbidity, and restricting the passage of toxic pollution and heavy metals.

At the San Francisco utility headquarters, similar water cleansing actions take place within the wastewater system called the Living Machine, created by Living Machine Systems. According to the company website, the Living Machine "blends cutting-edge science and engineering with plants and beneficial bacteria to efficiently treat and reuse wastewater, providing lasting water solutions for communities everywhere."[25]

GREEN ROOFS

The water-sustaining benefits of green roofs are well known; gardens on rooftops can capture 75 percent of the rain that would otherwise become runoff in gutters and sewers. Green roofs also add to a building's energy efficiency. The soil and plants add a thick layer of insulation that keeps buildings cooler in the summer and warmer in the winter. And gardens provide habitat for birds and insects.

The green roofs on the California Pacific Medical Center Van Ness Campus in San Francisco are models of water sustainability. Five separate gardens crown the hospital, adding 25,000 square feet (2,323 sq. m) of green space to an urban location. The gardens host wildflowers and plants from shady oak woodlands and coastal meadows. The blooms attract bees and monarch butterflies. The green roofs also act as protection against storm water runoff. Rainwater is captured and used for drip irrigation of the gardens. Capturing the rainwater saves 180,000 gallons (681,374 L) of water a year that otherwise would have been sent into storm drains and sewers.

Every day, the Living Machine treats 5,000 gallons (18,927 L) of gray water and black water produced by the utility's nine hundred employees. The first step in the process removes raw sewage from the water as it flows into a tank that filters out solids and sludge. This waste is pumped into the city sewer lines. The remaining effluent flows into a series of large basins that look like planter boxes located next to the building. The basins hold aquatic plants and are filled with gravel that encourages the growth of helpful bacteria. The unique aspect of the Living Machine is the process that simulates the ebb and flow of the sea in tidal marshes. The wastewater is pumped into the basins from the bottom and drained back into a recirculation tank. This process occurs twelve times a day.

After the water is cleansed by the tidal motions, it is sent to what is called the polishing vertical flow wetlands. During this step the effluent drips down through a gravel bed from the top. The gravel filters out remaining organic material and chemicals like ammonia and dissolved solids. The water is then filtered, exposed to UV light, and lightly chlorinated. The final product is stored in a recycled-water tank and is used for flushing the SFPUC facility's toilets. The Living Machine reduces total water use in the SFPUC headquarters by 65 percent.

Making Cities Sustainable

In 2017 there were only ten Living Buildings in the world, but those structures provide proof that net zero water use is achievable. And scientists have discovered that human technology intermingled with ecological systems can provide a step toward the goal of making cities sustainable. Green roofs topped with gardens filter rainwater just as the soil does in nature. Bioswales and Living Machines clean wastewater like ponds and wetlands do. There is little doubt that urban areas can be designed more like natural ecosystems. By following nature's lead, scientists are finding that buildings, roads, and cities can produce water that is sweet, clean, and sustainable.

SOURCE NOTES

Introduction: Sustainable Water

1. Quoted in Joseph Erbentraut, "Safe Tap Water Takes a Lot of Work," *Huffington Post*, November 17, 2016. www.huffing tonpost.com.
2. Quoted in James Stafford, "The Game-Changing Water Revolution: Interview with Stanley Weiner," OilPrice.com, April 13, 2015. http://oilprice.com.

Chapter One: The Science of Freshwater

3. Melissa Mays, "Flint Mom Shares the Heartbreak of Giving Her Kids Poison Water," *Huffington Post*, February 1, 2016. www.huffingtonpost.com.
4. Quoted in Adam Wernick, "An Investigation Has Found Lead in 2,000 Water Systems," PRI, April 9, 2016. www.pri.org.

Chapter Two: Reusing Wastewater

5. Quoted in Monte Morin, "Turning Sewage into Drinking Water Gains Appeal as Drought Lingers," *Los Angeles Times*, May 24, 2015. www.latimes.com.
6. Quoted in Anne C. Mulkern, "Californians Tap Technology—and Psychology—to Stretch Water Supplies," E&E News, May 12, 2016. www.eenews.net.
7. Dan Theobald, "Microorganisms in Activated Sludge," *Water Technology*, June 23, 2014. www.watertechonline.com.
8. Quoted in Dawn Fallik, "This New Study Found More Drugs in Our Drinking Water than Anybody Knew," *New Republic*, December 10, 2013. https://newrepublic.com.
9. Quoted in Jeremy Allen, "Biochar Takes the Pharmaceuticals Out of Urine," *Chemistry World*, March 2017. www.chemistry world.com.

Chapter Three: Desalination

10. Quoted in Lucy Schouten, "Egypt Finds Way to Make Salt Water Drinkable with Half the Energy," *Christian Science Monitor*, October 28, 2015. www.csmonitor.com.

11. Quoted in Claudia Dreifus, "Using a Leadership Role to Put a Human Face on Science," *New York Times*, January 26, 2009. www.nytimes.com.

Chapter Four: Cleaning Up Polluted Water

12. Bruce Kania, "Harvesting as a Water-Quality Strategy," Floating Island International, March 3, 2016. www.floatingislandin ternational.com.
13. Quoted in Emily Anthes, "Nature's Water Purifiers Help Clean Up Lakes," BBC, September 26, 2012. www.bbc.com.
14. Quoted in Anthes, "Nature's Water Purifiers Help Clean Up Lakes."
15. Quoted in Lisa Zyga, "Microbots Can Clean Up Polluted Water," Phys.org, April 11, 2016. https://phys.org.
16. Quoted in Emil Venere, "New Environmental Cleanup Technology Rids Oil from Water," Phys.org, April 5, 2016. https:// phys.org.
17. Quoted in David Nield, "The Tiny Device Makes Water Drinkable in Just 20 Minutes," Science Alert, August 19, 2017. www.sciencealert.com.
18. Quoted in Nield, "The Tiny Device Makes Water Drinkable in Just 20 Minutes."

Chapter Five: Sustainable Water in Cities

19. Denis Hayes, "Better, Faster, More," Bullitt Center, 2013. www.bullittcenter.org.
20. Hayes, "Better, Faster, More."
21. Quoted in Bettina Boxall, "When It Rains, Los Angeles Sends Billions of Gallons of 'Free Liquid Gold' Down the Drain," *Los Angeles Times*, March 8, 2017. www.latimes.com.
22. Quoted in Boxall, "When It Rains, Los Angeles Sends Billions of Gallons of 'Free Liquid Gold' Down the Drain."
23. Quoted in Maria L. La Ganga, "Seattle's Bullitt Center Is Flush with Green Features, Including Toilets," *Los Angeles Times*, March 31, 2015. www.latimes.com.
24. Bullitt Center, "Waste Not . . . ," 2013. www.bullittcenter.org.
25. Living Machine Systems, "Living Machine Technology," 2012. www.livingmachines.com.

🔬 FIND OUT MORE

Books

Robert Gardner, *Experiments for Future Chemists*. New York: Enslow, 2016.

Stuart A. Kallen, *Global Access to Clean Water*. San Diego: ReferencePoint, 2017.

Russell Kuhtz, *Physical Science*. New York: Rosen Education Service, 2017.

Susan Nichols, ed., *The Politics of Water Scarcity*. Farmington Hills, MI: Greenhaven, 2017.

Bill Nye, *Unstoppable: Harnessing Science to Change the World*. New York: St. Martin's Griffin, 2016.

Websites

Bullitt Center Building (www.bullittcenter.org/building). This site provides a comprehensive overview of the power, water, and wastewater systems that allow Bullitt Center to claim the title of greenest commercial building in the world.

Circle of Blue (www.circleofblue.org). In 2000 journalists and scientists founded this website to provide information about the world water crisis and its relationship to food, energy, and health.

E&E News (www.eenews.net). This website covers current events of interest to the general public and to energy and environment professionals. The website contains sections like Energywire, Greenwire, and Climatewire that are dedicated to keeping up with the latest environmental news.

Fundamentals of Environmental Measurements (www.fondriest.com/environmental-measurements). This science-based site focuses on procedures used to measure and monitor water quality, pH, dissolved oxygen, and other factors in rivers, lakes, and other surface waters.

Science Buddies (www.sciencebuddies.org). This site features science project ideas and guides in areas such as freshwater chemistry, microbiology, and the environment. Sections feature blogs, project guides, science career information, and expert advice.

Tox Town (https://toxtown.nlm.nih.gov). This website provides a link between pollution, the environment, and public health with sections about wastewater treatment, agricultural and industrial runoff, and storm water and sewage problems. The site is divided into various regions so users can find information about their specific location.

Water Defense (https://waterdefense.org). Water Defense is an environmental group dedicated to clean water founded by actor Mark Ruffalo. The group's site has information about problems with the water supply, sustainable water practices, and freshwater technology.

Water.org (www.water.org). Cofounded by actor Matt Damon, Water.org focuses on water and sanitation problems in poor countries. Its website provides statistics, maps, photos, and videos that highlight the problems as well as offer solutions.

Internet Sources

Monte Morin, "Turning Sewage into Drinking Water Gains Appeal as Drought Lingers," *Los Angeles Times*, May 24, 2015. www.latimes.com/local/california/la-me-toilet-to-tap-20150525-story.html.

Adam Wernick, "An Investigation Has Found Lead in 2,000 Water Systems," PRI, April 9, 2016. www.pri.org/stories/2016-04-09/investigation-has-found-lead-2000-us-water-systems.

INDEX

PICTURE CREDITS

ABOUT THE AUTHOR

Stuart A. Kallen is the author of more than 350 nonfiction books for children and young adults. He has written on topics ranging from the theory of relativity to the art of electronic dance music. In addition, Kallen has written award-winning children's videos and television scripts. In his spare time he is a singer, songwriter, and guitarist in San Diego.